NARRATIVE WRITING

By Tara McCarthy

S C H O L A S T I C
PROFESSIONAL**B**OOKS

New York • Toronto • London • Auckland • Sydney

Cover design by Vincent Ceci and Jaime Lucero
Interior design by Vincent Ceci and Drew Hires
Interior illustrations by Drew Hires

ISBN 0-590-20937-X

TABLE OF CONTENTS

TO THE TEACHER

Everyone Loves a Good Story!

A narrative tells a story. Telling stories aloud is probably the oldest form of human discourse. The *oral* form comes so naturally to us that we tend to overlook the important ways in which it is different from a *written* narrative.

As we tell stories aloud in an informal setting, we tend to "hop around"; we may tell events out of order, leave out important steps, or fail to identify characters clearly. In a sense, all that is OK: our gestures, expressions, and tones of voice can carry a lot of information; and immediate feedback and questions from the listening audience allow us to go back and fill in the blanks.

However, the audience expects and needs more from a *written* narrative. The story can't simply be "talk written down." All the essentials must be provided in an organized way. Whether the story is a one-paragraph true-life anecdote or a 600-page novel, it must have a central idea, characters, a plotline, adequate description, and usually a culminating event.

This book suggests strategies and activities for helping your students draw on their natural enthusiasm for story-telling in order to *write* narratives that satisfy both themselves and their reading audience.

BOOK EMPHASES

EMPHASIS ON PREWRITING AND EXPLORING

Because we learn to write by writing, every writer needs as many opportunities as possible to "just write" and to explore a variety of formats. Each of the first four sections of this book suggests several writer-ly approaches for the student to freely experiment with before he or she chooses a *particular* way to do the final writing assignment. The Culminating Activity in each section presents this assignment and briefly suggests drafting, conferencing, editing, and publishing options.

EMPHASIS ON WRITER-DIRECTED FEEDBACK

Writers most benefit from testing-out their ideas and drafts with an audience when **the writer is in command of that audience.** For example, a writer may simply wish to read a draft aloud to a small audience to hear what his or her written work sounds like, without comment from the listeners. Or, the writer may ask the audience to listen/read for, then comment on, a specific aspect of the draft such as **action** or **character development**. By using strategies like Free Read, Say-Back, Writer's Right, and Mental Movies, writers get the help they specifically want, while the audience develops skills in directed listening/reading.

EMPHASIS ON INTEGRATED COMPOSITION SKILLS

The eight Composition Skills lessons/reproducibles are introduced at point-of-contact, that is, where they are most relevant to students' needs as they draft, revise, and edit.

GENERAL TEACHING SUGGESTIONS

USE WRITING FOLDERS

Ask each student to make a separate writing folder for each of the first four sections. Explain that these folders are not Portfolios, representing "best" work. On the contrary, they are the writer's stockpile of *all* of her or his ideas and trial-runs for the section. For easy-reference purposes, supply students with gummed tags to briefly label each item in the folder, for example, (for Part I), *My Observation Diary, Partner Journal and Story Idea, Imagination Diary, Some events I could follow with a Log, People who have influenced me.* Also explain that the reason for keeping all ideas is that "You never know...!" An idea that seems lame or incomplete at first may eventually turn out to be the little gem that sparks a great piece of writing.

USE THE QUICKWRITES

The quickwrite strategy, now used in many writing programs, is proving to be a warm-up that not only engenders ideas but also shows even the most recalcitrant, doubtful student that he or she *can* actually *write.* You'll note that a Quickwrite is—as its name implies—a timed exercise based on a broad subject. For students, you might compare a Quickwrite to the stretching exercises a runner does before a race. Also assure students that no one is going to read the Quickwrite product unless the writer chooses to share it.

FEEL FREE TO PRESENT ACTIVITIES IN YOUR OWN WAY

If you wish, you can assign activities in different sections to appeal to different students' abilities and interests. Examples: (1) You may decide to move your visually oriented student immediately from Observation Diaries in Part 1 to Picture-Prompt Narratives in Part 2, to Making Illustrations in Part 4. (2) Students who are enthusiastically studying a particular historical figure might start with First-Person Biographies Based on History in Part 2, move on to Narrating Personal Connections in Part 3, then use the Partner-Journal approach in Part 1 to share ideas with a classmate.

No matter which sequence you decide to use, the activities will help students to practice the fundamentals of writing narratives and then to effectively apply what they learn to create good stories that everyone loves.

PART ONE

WRITING NARRATIVES ABOUT OUR OWN EXPERIENCES

GETTING STARTED

Almost every day, students narrate aloud many stories based on their personal experiences, often beginning with tried-and-true story-openers like these: "Guess what happened to me on the way to school!" "That reminds me of the time when..." "I know someone who..." "I had a dream about..." "What would happen if....?" "Have you heard what happened to (X)? He ..."

Because telling about our own experiences orally is such a natural part of our everyday lives, *writing* about these experiences makes a comfortable introduction to written narration in general. The activities in this section ease students into narrative writing through encouraging them to focus on what they know best: themselves.

TEACH SKILLS

You may want to integrate the following Composition Skills into this section: Strong Verbs (page 54); Precise Nouns (page 55); Transitional Words (page 56).

START-UP QUICKWRITE

Purpose: Helps each student to see that her or his experiences may be of interest to other people. Good strategy to use with "but-I-haven't-got-anything-to-write-about" students!

Students work in groups of four or five.

Directions: *You have three minutes. Make a list of interesting things that **other** members of your group have done or experienced.*

Follow-Up: Each student reads her or his list aloud. Group members tell what more they'd like to know about the experiences.

THREE WAYS OF JOURNALING

The word *journal* derives from a word meaning *day*. But in modern times, a journal is thought of not so much as a day-by-day report of one's activities but rather as one's personal account of really special events and insights, however often they occur. For writers, journal entries are raw material for longer narratives. Encourage your students to set up and keep journals using one or more of the suggested forms.

DOUBLE-ENTRY JOURNAL

Purpose: Promotes writing fluency in a non-threatening way; allows students to explore ideas that they may use later in narratives.

Show students how to set up double-column pages. On the left side, Fact: the student writes a fact about something that has happened to him or her, or about an event in a book the student is reading (*note-taking*). In the right-hand column, My Reaction: the student notes his or her feeling or opinion about the event (*note-making*).

FACT	MY REACTION
My grandfather gave his war medals to me!	I was upset. I hoped he'd give the medals to a museum.
Tom Sawyer tricked his friends into whitewashing the fence for him.	I think Tom was smart. The job got done. But I wonder if Tom would like his friends to trick him!
My mom took me and my brother to an art exhibit.	I thought I'd be bored, but I wasn't. The exhibit was of mobiles about circuses!

➤ *Writing Prompt!*
Tell your Fact and your Reaction in a paragraph. Add details.

PROBLEM-SOLUTION JOURNAL

Purpose: Encourages stating an initial situation clearly and then exploring possible outcomes

In the left column, the student states a real-life problem or a problem in a book he or she is reading. In the right column, the student writes one or more ways the problem might be solved.

PROBLEM

Our class has to read poems in a program for the whole school. The problem is that some kids get nervous when they have to speak to a large group.

We're just looking at the first part of the ODYSSEY, where Ulysses is returning from the Trojan Wars. The problem is that Ulysses gets lost and can't find his way home!

POSSIBLE SOLUTIONS

Shy kids could participate by making posters or pictures about the poems classmates will read. Shy kids could practice reading a poem to just a few of us and then to more and more of us.

Maybe Ulysses could just anchor his ship and wait for a captain of another ship to come along and give him directions. He could beg the goddess Athena to get him home safely.

➤ *Writing Prompt!*
Write about what would happen if one of your Possible Solutions was put into action.

PARTNER JOURNAL

Purpose: Provides a nonjudgmental way for students to compare reactions to real-life events and events in literature

Show students how to set up three-column pages. In the first column, the student states a fact about an event in real life or in a book. In the second column, the student writes his or her reactions to or predictions about the event. In the third column, the student's partner responds to the note in Columns 1 and 2.

SITUATION	MY NOTES	MY PARTNER'S IDEAS
Our school building is so crowded that we had to divide the gym into classrooms!	I don't think this is fair! Now we have no place for indoor games and sports.	I don't think it's fair, either! Could we ask the PTA to find a nearby space for kids to use?
In MARTHA SPEAKS, a dog eats alphabet soup, and then she can talk as humans do.	I like this idea! I've always wondered what dogs would say if they could speak like we do.	I think a better idea would be for humans to learn dog-talk. The humans could eat dog biscuits and then communicate as dogs do.

➤ *Writing Prompt!*

Make more columns for your Partner Journal. You can add a column called My Reaction to My Partner's Ideas. The next column might be More Ideas from My Partner.

WRITING PROCESS IDEA: BRAINSTORM WITH YOURSELF!

Encourage students to review their journals at least once a week to jot down any story ideas they get from reviewing the entries. Explain that story-idea notes can be phrases, informal lists, or sentences, but should always present events in time-sequence.

Example (from Partner Journal):

A STORY IDEA

1. I eat a dog biscuit.

2. Now I can discuss things with my dog in dog-talk.

3. In dog-talk, my dog alerts me to a danger to my family.

4. My dog and I save my family!

OBSERVATION DIARIES

Purpose: Encourages students to observe changes or sequences of events and to narrate them in a bare-bones way

In an Observation Diary, the writer chooses an object or nonhuman entity in his or her immediate environment and notes briefly, over a two- or three-day period, what happens to the object or how it changes. (Because the Observation Diary doesn't focus on the student's personal life as a traditional diary does, entries can be shared without raising "invasion of privacy" issues.)

Help students get started by explaining what an Observation Diary is and providing a sample entry via chalkboard or overhead.

OBSERVING MY PENCIL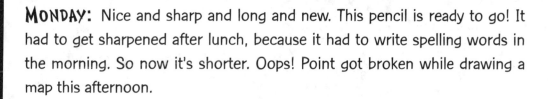

MONDAY: Nice and sharp and long and new. This pencil is ready to go! It had to get sharpened after lunch, because it had to write spelling words in the morning. So now it's shorter. Oops! Point got broken while drawing a map this afternoon.

TUESDAY: Pencil got lost in my desk for a while. Found under a pile of old lunch bags. Pencil looks stubby, and there is peanut butter on it.

WEDNESDAY: Sharpened pencil. But what happened to the eraser end? Now it's stubby! Pencils require a lot of attention!

Have the class brainstorm for a chalkboard list of objects or animals they might observe. Then ask each student to choose an item from the list to write about over in an observation diary.

- a tree outside your window
- a household pet
- your toothbrush
- the morning sky
- a classroom aquarium
- birds at a birdfeeder
- your favorite shoes
- sounds in your neighborhood

- a junk car in an empty lot
- the school corridor
- an ant colony, a spider web
- a swing on the playground
- the school gym
- a table in the classroom
- the sun, stars, moon
- a particular sidewalk or street

WRITING PROCESS IDEA: DRAFT, THEN READ ALOUD

Ask students to use their diary entries to write a brief paragraph that narrates sequentially what they've observed. Then have students form small Free-Read groups. In a FreeRead, the writer reads aloud to the group. Group members listen but don't comment. While or just after reading, the writer makes notes about what he or she would like to change in or add to the draft. Example:

MY PARAGRAPH	MY NOTES
On Monday, the pencil was brand new.	Add yellow, long, pointy.
I used it to write spelling notes, so it got stubby. Then the point broke while I was drawing a map. I stuck the pencil away in my desk, where it fell under some old lunch bags and got smeared with peanut butter. On Wednesday morning, I found the pencil, but the eraser was stubby!	Idea: I wonder how a pencil would feel if it could feel things. Add "Tuesday," to show the sequence. Idea: I wonder what words the eraser erased!
How did that happen?	If a pencil could think, would it remember?

Via Free Reads, students learn more about writing than they do from any other strategy.

➤ **Writing Prompt!**
Try rewriting your paragraph, using the notes you made during your Free Read.

LOGS

Purpose: Helps students focus on exactly what they find out about a subject and then narrate their findings in sequence

Keeping an Observation Diary is an open-ended writing activity: The writer doesn't know beforehand exactly what specific details she or he will be telling about the chosen subject. Keeping a log, on the other hand, is a closure activity: Writers narrate in time-sequence information that applies only to a specific situation or task that has been defined beforehand.

Explain what a log is. List people who routinely keep logs and have students determine the major questions each example log-keeper wishes to answer. For example: (*Ship captain*) What progress does my ship make day-by-day? (*School nurse*) What students came to my office today, and what were their problems? (*Building guard*) Who wanted to enter the building tonight, and what was their purpose and my response?

On the chalkboard or on an overhead projector, show the following log. Ask students to note the title and to read the entries aloud. Then ask students to tell what sequence the log uses (time sequence). Ask: How would this chart help a writer write a story about the hurricane?

LOG: What Happens as the Hurricane Approaches Our Town?

6 A.M.: Weather forecasters say hurricane will hit our area in about five hours. Homeowners and storekeepers hammer up shields for windows and doors.

7 A.M.: Strong winds are kicking up. Big waves hit beaches. Sun hidden as clouds move in fast.

7:30 A.M.: Local radio advises people to move inland to shelters. Police and firefighters go house-to-house to warn residents.

8:30 A.M.: Hurricane approaching faster than predicted! People along the shoreline being evacuated fast. Flood conditions all along our coast. High winds topple trees.

9 A.M.: I go with my family to a shelter in a school about 15 miles inland. A lot of people are scared. Some of us think it's real exciting!

10 A.M.:	Electric power out. Battery radio at shelter. We learn that the hurricane is affecting all of the East Coast.
11 A.M.:	High winds howling all around this shelter. But radio reports storm is turning north-northeast and will leave our area in four or five hours and blow out to sea.

Have the class brainstorm a chalkboard list of subjects that invite regular log entries over a period of a week or two. Ask students to work independently or with a partner or small group to choose a subject, prepare a log notebook, and write entries at regular intervals. Point out that each entry should begin with the time or date on which the event happens.

Sample Brainstorm List:
- weather conditions over a week's time
- the progress of a class project
- the development of a newborn sibling
- personal reactions to a novel or chapter book being read over a period of days
- the progress of a community project such as planning a street fair or setting up a soup kitchen
- steps taken to carry out a long-range homework assignment or independent project
- steps taken in getting to know a new classmate
- a day-by-day account of moving into a new neighborhood or school

WRITING PROCESS IDEA: DRAFT A PARAGRAPH

Ask students to use their log entries to write one or more paragraphs about the subject. You may wish to show a model paragraph based on the sample log:

WHAT HAPPENED AS A HURRICANE APPROACHED OUR TOWN

It started with a 6 A.M. warning from weather forecasters that the hurricane would soon hit our town. Right away, homeowners and storekeepers began to hammer up shields for windows and doors. Soon after that, at about 7 A.M., strong winds kicked up, big waves hit the beaches, and storm clouds covered the sun. Then radio announcers, police, and firefighters warned people along the shore to move to inland shelters.

► **Writing Prompt!**

If you haven't got any ideas yet for your own log narrative, practice with the log entries we've studied about the hurricane. Write another paragraph about what happens from 9 A.M. to 11 A.M.

AUTOBIOGRAPHICAL INCIDENTS

Purpose: Helps students examine an experience and discover what they've learned from it

An autobiographical incident narrates a personal experience that occurred over a brief span of time: within a few minutes, a few hours, or—at most—over a day or two. Like most narratives, the autobiographical incident presents events in sequence. To this sequential narration, the writer adds her or his sensory impressions, and shares her or his feelings with the reader.

Explain what an autobiographical incident is. Stress that it doesn't deal with some earth-shaking, newspaper-worthy public event but rather with an event that is important to the *writer*.

To help students understand that brief, simple incidents can affect you strongly, recount such an incident from your own life. Example:

Outside the house where we lived when I was a little girl, there was a birch tree that had been bent over by many winter storms. In the summer, the leaves of the bending tree trailed on the ground and formed a little tent. I called it my Reading Tree, because I would sit under the leafy boughs and read my books. It was a green, cool, and private place, and I loved it very much.

One summer day, I came home from a picnic with my friends—and my Reading Tree was gone! All that as left was a short, sawed-off, sad-looking stump! I burst into tears. My dad came running out of the house. "What's the matter?" he said. "My Reading Tree! My Reading Tree!" I bawled, pointing to the stump. "Oh, Sweetie," my father said, "we had to have it cut down because it was full of a tree-disease that could infect other trees. You understand that, don't you?" "Yes, Dad," I said. But I really didn't understand then. And even now—when I do understand—I still miss my Reading Tree.

Ask each student to jot subjects or titles for three or four autobiographical incidents. Present some examples to show how informally these subjects/titles can be recorded:

- new school; I was scared; then met new friend
- the day I got my puppy
- lost in the shopping mall when I was 4 years old

➤ *Writing Prompt!*
For students who need more help in stirring up memories and feelings that they can use to write autobiographical incidents, try the following prompts. After each, provide time for students to respond through pictures or through brief, written phrases.

- Close your eyes. See a "still-life" or photo from your past. People and objects are frozen in time. Now tell what your still-life shows.

- Close your eyes. See a moving picture from your past as if you're watching a movie or a TV show. Now tell what your moving picture shows.

- Close your eyes. I'll say four words that name feelings. Flash on incidents in your life when you've had these feelings. (*sad; puzzled; happy; angry*) Now tell about the time when you had one of these feelings.

WRITING PROCESS IDEA:
REVISE FOR SEQUENCE

Ask students to write rough drafts of an autobiographical incident. Have writing partners check one another's drafts for *sequence*. Are the events told in the order in which they happened? Are there places where transitional words and phrases would help the reader follow the sequence? (Refer students to page 56.)

ACTIVITIES

FRIENDLY LETTERS
Suggest that students narrate a recent autobiographical incident as part of a letter to a friend or relative.

CLASS REPORTS
Suggest that as a follow-up to a field trip or science investigation, students write a sequential narrative about the experience.

IMAGINATION DIARIES
Ask students to project themselves ten or twenty years into the future. Ask them to write journal or diary entries based on what they predict or imagine themselves doing in this future time.

POSTCARD MINI-NARRATIVES

Use postcards of your community or state, or repros of photos of local sites or of your own class's trips or projects as materials. Ask students to use scrap paper to rough-draft three or four sentences that narrate in sequence an event related to the picture and then to write the proofread sentences as the postcard message. Encourage students to address and send their postcards.

CULMINATING ACTIVITY: WRITING ABOUT OURSELVES

Ask students to go through their Writing Folders to select the piece they will carry through to completion via the writing process. A writer may wish to talk with you, a partner, or a small group about *why* he or she likes a particular piece, but the final choice must be the writer's.

Final products may represent all the forms suggested in this unit: journal entries, imaginative stories, logs, autobiographical incidents, etc. In addition some students may wish to accompany their narratives with photos, drawings, maps, or other graphics

During the revision and editing steps, partners may wish to pay special attention to the Composition Skills you've reviewed with the class.

Encourage students to publish their work by tape-recording it, by forming discussion groups around common topics represented in their writing, or by performing pantomimes or skits.

Remind students to keep all the ideas for Writing About Our Own Experiences. These ideas will often inspire or enrich additional ones.

PART TWO

WRITING NARRATIVES ABOUT OTHER PEOPLE

GETTING STARTED

An other-oriented focus is a vital one for young writers. On both an affective and a cognitive level, the focus helps students appreciate the views and situations of real people with whom they come in contact in everyday life or in their curricular studies of the past. On an imaginative level, the focus encourages students to trust and use their writerly, "what-if" instincts to try a variety of points-of-view as they develop their own stories.

TEACH SKILLS

You may want to integrate the following Composition Skills into this section: Transitional Words (page 56); Combining Sentences (page 57).

START-UP QUICKWRITE

Purpose: Helps students focus on people that interest them. Here's a useful warm-up for all students.

*You have five minutes. Imagine that you're stranded on a desert island with just **one** other person. It can be a person from history or someone you know personally. Tell who this person is and list at least three reasons why you choose her or him as your desert-island companion.*

FIRST-PERSON BIOGRAPHIES

Purpose: Encourages students to focus on interactions: how one character influences another

A first-person biography narrates an incident involving the writer and someone she or he knows personally. An exemplary first-person biography shows something important about the focus character *and* shows how this character has affected the writer's life or ideas.

Help students get started by explaining what a first-person biography is and providing an example via an overhead or hand-outs of the following:

Mr. Ames

Mr. Ames is known as the Neighborhood Grouch. He never answers when you speak to him. He always has a sort of frown on his face. He lives alone and never seems to have visitors.

"Mr. Ames is just so *unfriendly*," said my Mom.

"He's a total drag!" said my sister.

Describes the main character

One day, my Frisbee landed accidentally in Mr. Ames's garden. He was working out there, so I was a little afraid of retrieving the Frisbee.

Then Mr. Ames held up the Frisbee. "Here's your toy, Sonny," he said. He was smiling slightly.

"Thanks!" I said as I went to get the Frisbee. "I'm usually pretty good at aiming these things, but a slight breeze can throw them off-course."

"Eh? Eh?" said Mr. Ames, cupping his hand to his ear.

Narrates the interaction between main character and writer

Suddenly I realized that Mr. Ames was totally deaf! No wonder he didn't reply to neighbors' greetings! No wonder he seemed unfriendly! He couldn't hear us!

That day I not only got my Frisbee back but also stayed to help Mr. Ames set in tomato plants. We communicated just fine through gestures and smiles.

So I learned that you can't always rely on other people's opinions. Often you have to check things out for yourself and form your own ideas. My idea of Mr. Ames is that he's a great guy and a good friend!

Tells what the writer has learned from the interaction

Have students work independently to list family members, friends, teachers, neighbors, or people encountered by chance who have affected or influenced their views. Then have students work with a partner or small group to tell *when*, *why* or *how* these persons influenced them.

WRITING PROCESS IDEA: SAY-BACK

Ask students to rough-draft a first-person biography. Assure students that the only standard here is that the draft be neat and clear enough for the writer to read it smoothly to an audience of four or five classmates.

Instruct students how to use a Say-Back Response: The writer reads her or his draft, then asks the audience to "say-back" in their own words what the writer is getting at. Writer's questions: "What do you hear me saying? What are some ideas you have for helping me say it better?"

> *Say-backs are valuable when students are at the early stages of framing a narrative and are looking for a main idea to center on.*

➤ *Writing Prompt!*
Try rewriting your first-person biography, using the say-back comments of your classmates.

Try this with students who are having trouble with writing first-person autobiographies. Write a thank-you letter to the person who has influenced you. Tell what you have learned and why you are thankful.

FIRST-PERSON NARRATIVES BASED ON HISTORY

Purpose: Helps students to understand the feelings and motives of other people and to implement these understandings in writing narratives

Through basal texts and related literature, your students encounter real-life people of the past whose exploits and achievements have a global significance. What can an "ordinary" person possibly share with these historical giants? Students can find out by composing brief narratives in which they take on the "I" persona of a historical figure.

Introduce the concept by reading aloud a statement that might have been made by a historical person your students are studying. Ask the class to guess the identity. Example:

You think it's easy to follow familiar paths? Not if it's slave territory! Believe me, I quaked every step of every journey! I could be intercepted, captured, punished, returned to a slave's life at any time! You can call me courageous if you want. But I didn't feel *courageous*. I felt *determined*. I was determined to lead as many of my people as possible from slavery to freedom. But it was a scary task, every step of the way!

Harriet Tubman

Have students brainstorm to complete a chart that briefly notes major situations faced by real-life persons they've recently studied. Note that the My Situation column states the situations in the first-person, as they might have been seen by the characters themselves.

REAL-LIFE PERSON	MY SITUATION
Christopher Columbus	My crew threatens mutiny! We have been at sea for many weeks, and there's no land in sight!
Chief Joseph of the Nez Perce	The invaders move closer. I must lead my people to safety. But can the little children survive a long, cold journey on foot?
Amelia Earhart	Flying west over the Pacific Ocean. My co-pilot and I have never felt so lost and alone.

WRITING PROCESS IDEA: VISUALIZATION

Ask students to rough draft a paragraph or two based on one of the chart entries. The rough draft should add details that describe the character's situation more fully than the chart does. Then have students form small groups and read their paragraphs aloud. Groups can use the Free-Read strategy (see page 12) or try Mental Movies: while the writer reads aloud, listeners close their eyes and envision what the words make them see. Listeners then tell what they saw in their Mental Movies. Listeners make no other comments than that, however!

Mental Movies (1) give the writer feedback about how well his or her piece of writing is conveying the desired message; (2) provide ideas about how to enrich the piece of writing.

➤ *Writing Prompt!*
Make a second draft of your first-person narrative, using the ideas you got from your Free Read or from your group's Mental Movies.

IF ONLY THEY COULD SPEAK! UNUSUAL NARRATORS

Purpose: Helps students expand and employ their understanding of point-of-view. What did Amelia Earhart's plane feel like? What did Columbus's *Santa Maria* think as it was tossed about on the wild Atlantic? What thoughts might the hidden paths and safe houses have thought as they were used by the people Tubman guided to freedom? Though such questions may seem bizarre, they are extremely useful to young writers as they practice seeing events and people from different points of view. A classic example is Robert Lawson's *Ben and Me*, in which a mouse in Benjamin Franklin's house tells about (and takes credit for!) a number of Franklin's inventions.

Introduce the concept by having students brainstorm a list of pets, things, and places that they interact with or use almost every day.

my cat Mitzie	the school bus	my lunch box
the gym	Twiggy, our class hamster	the refrigerator
the water fountain	the local mall	my school desk
my running shoes	my dogs, Herman and Footie	the TV set

Next, say aloud to the class some statements that might be made by one of the chart "speakers," if indeed it could speak. Have students identify the speaker. Example:

THE REFRIGERATOR

Open, close! Open, close! On and off goes my light! These people are always looking for stuff to eat! And then I have to listen to all their questions and complaints! "Who ate all the peanut butter?" "There's nothing good in here for a snack!" Well, it's not my fault that the family's too busy to stock me up with goodies! Open my door! Slam it shut! How I love the hours after midnight when they've all gone to sleep and I get a little peace and quiet. Then I can discuss life with the ice cubes or tell bedtime stories with the milk carton and the margarine.

With you as scribe at the chalkboard, the whole class can draft a paragraph told from the first-person point of view of another item on their brainstormed list. As students work along, intercede as necessary to remind them: "You are telling this from someone else's point of view. Imagine that you are this other "someone." How would this "other someone" say it?" Point out where the words I, me, my, mine establish the first-person point of view.

WRITING PROCESS IDEA: COMBINE TWO APPROACHES

Have the class brainstorm again to list things that were—or *might* have been—involved with the real-life persons they've explored previously. In addition to Earhart's plane, Columbus's ship, and Tubman's safe havens, these might include:

Paul Revere's horse

Thomas Edison's first lightbulb

A pen used by Edgar Allan Poe

Sojourner Truth's cat

Mary Shelley's desk where she wrote "Frankenstein"

Sacajawea's canoe as she guided explorers through the Northwest

The Hudson River as ships from Europe begin to explore it

A dinosaur fossil as it's dug up by a paleontologist

Ask students to work independently or with a writing partner to choose one of the non-human entities and write about the historical incident from its first-person point of view. Suggest that writers use the Say-Back strategy (see page 21) as a way of sharing and getting valuable feedback to use in a second draft.

➤ *Writing Prompt!*
   What would you like to change in your draft? Make notes in the margin.

PICTURE-PROMPT NARRATIVES

Purpose: Helps students to create imaginative narratives

You can use great photos and reproductions of fine art to stimulate students' narrative imagination. Choose newspaper and magazine photos that show people in action or exhibiting strong feelings (for example, curiosity, joy, anger). Search through your library's art-collection books for paintings that do the same. For example, there's mystery in Henri Rousseau's "The Sleeping Gypsy," adventure and danger in Winslow Homer's "The Gulf Stream," peace and order in Georges Seurat's "A Sunday Afternoon at La Grande Jatte." If the atmosphere, action, and human emotion in a picture are exciting to *you*, your students will undoubtedly catch your enthusiasm.

Display the photos and paintings. (Include artists' names and picture titles whenever possible.) Model the activity by telling a brief story that one of the pictures inspires. Example:

This is a painting by Edouard Degas. It shows a ballet dancer lacing up her shoe. Here's the story *I* imagine:

> The dancer's name is Sophie. She's very nervous! This will be her first time in a public performance. All her family and friends are in the audience. Sophie wonders, "Will I be OK? Will I make every step right?" Sophie goes onstage. She is perfect! She bows and smiles. "This is the life for me!" she says to herself.

Ask student partners to choose a picture from the display, discuss what it shows, and share ideas about the story or stories it suggests. Partners can make notes in chart form. Example:

Title of Painting: "Coyote Meets the Lone Ranger in a Painted Desert"
Artist: Harry Fonseca

What It Shows	**Ideas for Stories**
The Lone Ranger is looking straight ahead. He doesn't seem to see the desert or Coyote.	Maybe the Lone Ranger has gotten lost in the desert. Coyote will guide him back to town.
The desert is full of color. The sky is blue. Coyote is wearing a biker jacket and sunglasses. He is grinning as he looks at the Lone Ranger.	Coyote may think that the Lone Ranger is pretty silly not to be looking around at the beautiful desert. Coyote will give him a guided tour!
He looks sort of fierce!	Maybe Coyote considers the Lone Ranger an invader and will chase him away.

WRITING PROCESS IDEA:
ASK FOR THE FEEDBACK YOU WANT

Ask students to write short narratives based on the charts they made with their partners. Remind students to refer to the picture itself for additional ideas. Then have partners read their drafts to one another. Suggest that partners use the Writer's Right strategy: the author gives the audience an assignment by telling them exactly what to listen for. Examples: "I'd like you to listen to the descriptions in my story." "Please listen for the actions (plot) in my story." "There are two characters in my story. Please listen to find out what they're like." Listeners then provide only the feedback the writer has asked for.

➤ *Writing Prompt!*

If your listener gave you some useful feedback, use it to make changes in your draft.

- Writer's Right is especially helpful to students who have undertaken the same writing assignment and thus understand the particular challenges of that assignment.

ACTIVITIES

HISTORY LETTERS

Ask students to imagine that two real-life persons from different eras of history, but with common interests, could correspond with one another. For example, what events might Meriwether Lewis and a modern astronaut tell one another about in an exchange of letters about *exploring*? What events might Harriet Tubman and Dr. Martin Luther King relate to one another?

HISTORY NEWSPAPERS

If your class is studying a particular historical era or location, have students work in small groups to write newspaper narratives about key events of the time. These should be presented as if they're hot news! Spur ideas with sample headlines:

PHARAOH COMPLAINS ABOUT SLOW PACE OF PYRAMID CONSTRUCTION.

NILE FLOODS RIGHT ON TIME!

NEFERTITI ASCENDS THRONE TO CHEERS

RIGHT-NOW MAGAZINE STORIES

Suggest to students that they write news-notes or brief narratives about their school and neighborhoods to compile into a weekly periodical. Spur ideas with magazine titles based on ones kids know: **People** at Chapman School, **Time** for Us, Our **News** This **Week**.

NARRATIVE POETRY

Many of your students may enjoy exploring this way of telling stories, especially if you introduce the activity by reading aloud some examples: golden oldies like the Robin Hood ballads or some of Shel Silverstein's humorous modern poetry-stories.

CULMINATING ACTIVITY: WRITING ABOUT OTHER PEOPLE

As a class warm-up, ask each student to carefully look through his or her Writing Folder for this unit, then call out one or two favorite titles and/or descriptions of drafts and notes in the folder. List these on the chalkboard. Examples:

my first-person biography about my grandmother	"A Ship Speaks" (a narrative told by the **Titanic**)
my first-person history narrative: Emma Goldman tells about writing the poem for the Statue of Liberty	"Dog Explorer" (an incident reported by Meriwether Lewis's dog)
letters exchanged by Pocahontas and Sacajawea	"Fighting Sharks" (told from the point of view of a a sailor shown in the painting "The Gulf Stream")
narrative poem: "The Ballad of Crazy Horse"	History Newspaper article: "Aztecs Battle Invaders"

Encourage the class to comment on what they find interesting about each entry on the brainstormed list. (This strategy provides useful input for the individual writer.)

Have each pupil fully develop a piece from his or her Writing Folder, choose a writing partner, and follow the usual writing-process steps. During the revision and editing steps, have partners pay special attention to the Composition Skills you've reviewed with the class.

Have students work in large groups (eight to ten members) to decide on a way to publish their final products. Categorized anthologies? TV shows in which the authors (real or imaginary) are interviewed? Read-alouds for family guests?

Some students will enjoy a metacognitive round-up in which they discuss the most difficult and the most fun aspects of writing narratives about other people. The round-up can be presented as a panel presentation before a classroom audience.

PART THREE

WRITING NARRATIVES ABOUT LITERATURE

GETTING STARTED

Writing a narrative about a particular book or story encourages students to think like the author did, to get into that author's shoes by extending or elaborating on the existing narrative. The approach is similar to the one an art student uses: She or he sets up an easel before a great painting, replicates or reinterprets it, and in that way learns the techniques used by the artist.

You'll note that writing a narrative about literature is quite different from writing a report about literature. A report comes at a book from the "outside," from the reader's critical stance.

A narrative about a book comes from the "inside," from the student writer's participation in the story.

TEACH SKILLS

You may want to integrate the following Composition Skills into this section: Comparisons (page 58); Punctuating Conversation (page 59).

START-UP QUICKWRITE

Read aloud to the class an exciting passage from a novel or story. Then give these directions: "You have four minutes. Write down all the ideas and images that popped into your mind as you listened to this paragraph."

Purpose: Provides a warm-up for summarizing a story

STORY SUMMARIES

Purpose: Helps students recall major elements in a story

An exemplary story summary is brief. It states the main steps in the plot in sequence and names the main characters. Walking your class through "how to write a-summary" may be time-consuming, but it pays off in big ways later on, because it provides the background students need if they're to write independently about literature.

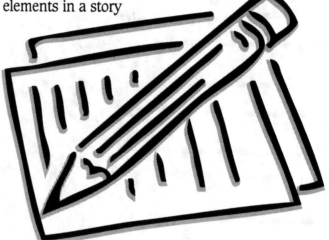

Start with a whole-class brainstorm: with you as scribe at the chalkboard, students describe briefly what happened in a story the class has read or heard. (Leave lots of space between each line of the chalkboard paragraph.) Then:

- The class decides what information in the paragraph is unnecessary or irrelevant. (Cross these phrases out.)
- The class studies the remaining information and determines if it's given in order. (Circle any phrases or sentences that are out of sequence and draw arrows to where they belong.)
- The class determines if any important plot information has been left out and whether all the key characters have been named. (Write any vital additions above the lines where they belong.)
- With your guidance, the class identifies places where key information can be stated in a briefer way. (This is an apt place for reviewing ways to combine sentences [page 57].)
- Read aloud the final version of the chalkboard summary. If possible, make a clean copy of it. Explain to the class what they've accomplished (a story summary) and help them list the criteria they've applied. Example:

A summary:

1. States only the *main events* and states them in the order they happened;
2. Includes the names of the main characters;
3. Combines ideas whenever possible;
4. Is short: gives all the essential information as briefly as possible.

If necessary, provide—via chalkboard or copies to distribute—a model summary. Ask the class to tell how it meets the criteria.

> Cinderella wants to go to the King's ball, but her sisters won't let her. Cinderella's godmother provides her with a dress and a carriage, and Cinderella goes to the ball. The Prince falls in love with her. Leaving the ball, Cinderella loses her glass slipper. The Prince searches everywhere for the woman whom the slipper will fit. He finally finds Cinderella. The shoe fits, and the Prince marries her.

Have the class brainstorm a list of titles of stories they've recently read. Then ask each student to work independently to choose one of the stories and rough-draft a summary of it.

The student then reads the draft to a partner who is not as familiar with the story. Partners can adapt the Say-Back strategy (see page 21). Here, the writer directs: "Say back to me in your own words (in order) the events I wrote about and the main characters I named."

WRITING PROCESS IDEA: USE THE SAY-BACK TO REVISE

Ask students to write second drafts of their story summaries on the basis of what they discovered in reading them aloud and in listening to the Say-Backs. Did you present steps clearly and in sequence? Did you give the exact names of the main characters involved in the events?

➤ *Writing Prompt!*
Write numerals (**1, 2, 3**, etc.) next to each event you tell about in your summary. Check to make sure this shows the order in which things really happened in the story. If an event is out of order in your summary, circle the sentence and use an arrow to show where it belongs.

BOOK CHARACTER CONVERSATIONS

Purpose: Encourages students to focus on characters

A book-character conversation is modeled on a TV interview show. Characters who appear in different stories but who have much in common are interviewed by a host (you, or—in a follow-up—a savvy student).

Get started with a chalkboard chart that notes a common characteristic of characters in different stories and relevant major questions the interviewer might ask. Encourage students to extend the chart with other characteristics (for example, fear, fun, friendship) and examples of characters from other stories who have these characteristics.

CHARACTERISTIC	INTERVIEWEES	INTERVIEWER'S PROMPTS
Courage	**Winnie-the-Pooh** who went up in a balloon to get honey **Sam** in *My Side of the Mountain*, who lived alone in the wilderness **Gretel** in "Hansel and Gretel," who fooled the witch and rescued her brother	What was courageous about what you did? What happened? What is your advice to someone who might want to try to same thing? Winnie, Sam, and Gretel, share with us your ideas about what courage is.

Invite groups of students to choose roles and act out the interviews they've outlined on their chart. Provide rehearsal time. If possible, tape-record the finished interviews and provide time for the class to listen to them. Directed-listening prompt: "Listen to discover what these book characters have in common, and how they are different."

WRITING PROCESS IDEA: DRAFT SOME DIALOGUE
Ask groups to present the high points of the interview conversation in written form. (This is an apt place for reviewing the mechanics of writing dialogue [page 59].)

DIFFERENT VOICES

Purpose: Helps students consider story events from the viewpoints of different characters in the story

In a well-told story, all the major characters come alive because the writer has thought deeply about what each of them is *like*. When young writers emulate this valuable prewriting process, they not only gain insights into a book or story they've read but also find ways to develop and enrich their own stories.

Get started by reviewing with students a story they've read which is told from the first-person point of view (*I*). An example is Edgar Allan Poe's story

"The Fall of the House of Usher." Point out that all the events in the story are recounted from the "I" viewpoint of the man who visits the gloomy home of Roderick Usher, his boyhood friend. Ask students to consider scenes and events from the same story from the "I" viewpoints of Roderick or of Roderick's dying sister, Madeline. Present a model, then examples of retellings.

(Model, from the Poe story): The Visitor Speaks as "I."

"While he spoke, the Lady Madeline...passed through...and without having noticed my presence, disappeared. I regarded her with an utter astonishment not unmixed with dread....When a door...closed upon her, my glance sought instinctively and eagerly the countenance of the brother; but he had buried his face in his hands, and I could only perceive...the emaciated fingers through which trickled many passionate tears."

(Example #1) Roderick Usher speaks as "I."

How could I explain to my friend how despairing I was over my sister's illness? As she appeared in the doorway, I realized again how frail and sick she was. I began to weep as I thought how empty my life would be without her.

(Example #2) Madeline Usher speaks as "I."

Weak as I was, I still managed to get downstairs to peek at this visitor who had come to our house. I hoped he didn't see me! I knew I looked dreadfully ill. I returned to my room, comforted that my sad, lonely brother finally had a friend to talk to.

Ask the class to work together to retell another part of the sample story you've chosen from the "I" viewpoint of another character. Write the retelling on the chalkboard. As a metacognitive follow-up, encourage students to tell what they learn from looking at story incidents from different viewpoints—for example, feelings of the character, character's motives, details that only that character would know or care about.

Ask each student to choose a book she or he has read and narrate in a rough-draft paragraph a key event in the book from the "I" viewpoint of one of the characters. Examples: Fern, in *Charlotte's Web*, might speak as "I" as she tells about the amazing messages she reads in the spider web. Orville Wright, as portrayed in Russell Freedman's *The Wright Brothers: How They Invented the Airplane*, might speak as "I" as he tells about the excitement and wonder of flying a glider.

WRITING PROCESS IDEA: POINTING

Ask students to read their draft paragraphs to a group of four or five classmates. Before reading, the writer directs: "Listen, then tell me which of my words or phrases stick in your mind. Just tell me what they are; don't explain *why*."

> **Pointing** *helps a writer decide if the main viewpoint is getting through to the audience.*

 Writing Prompt!

Use what you learned from Pointing to write a second draft.

ADDING TO THE STORY

Most professional writers strive to show how one event flows believably from the events that precede it. By creating logical extensions of stories and books they've read, your students come to appreciate and use the task of plotting as they create their own stories.

NEW EPISODES

Purpose: Helps students focus on plot and the logical progression of story events

Lead the class through a Let's-Imagine activity to help students brainstorm what might happen to a favorite story character after the given story they've read is concluded. Examples: (1) Let's imagine that Wilbur, the pig in *Charlotte's Web*, has grow quite old and meets two new piglets in the farmyard. What might the new piglets think or worry about, and how might Wilbur help them? (2) Let's imagine that Rumplestiltskin, stomping down to the center of the earth after the queen has guessed his name, meets another magical being who wants to help a human complete a task. What might the task be? How might Rumplestiltskin help with the task, using the experience he had with the miller's daughter?

Ask students to work with a partner to think of and write notes or an outline about an episode that extends a story both partners are familiar with. Partners then (1) work independently to rough-draft the episode; (2) read their drafts to one another.

> **Writing Prompt!**
>
> Stuck for ideas about how to get going? Just *write*, like you do in a Quickwrite. Fast and furiously, write about all the things that might happen in this episode you and your partner have outlined or made notes about.

WRITING PROCESS IDEA: USE "SAY-BACK" AGAIN

In this context, the writer directs: "Listen for the events I tell about. When I finish reading, tell me the events in sequence. What are some ideas you have to help me make the sequence clearer?"

Ask students to use audience ideas to write a new draft of the episode.

PUT YOURSELF INTO THE STORY

Purpose: Helps students to develop empathy for the central characters in a story and an understanding of how events affect behavior

Have the class brainstorm for a three-column chalkboard chart. The first column names book characters they admire, the second column what admirable things the characters accomplished. Students suggest entries for the third column after they've discussed this situation: "Imagine that you are a new character in this story. You interact with the main character. You help him or her accomplish goals, or talk with the main character. You can refer to yourself as I, or use your real name." Sample chart:

Story and Main Character	Accomplishment	Me in the Story
Sam in *My Side of the Mountain*	Manages to live on his own in the wilderness for a whole year!	I meet Sam while I'm hiking. He agrees to let me share his wilderness adventure. I help Sam find food and build a shelter.
Billie Wind in *The Talking Earth*	Explores the Everglades, runs into many dangers, surmounts them all, and learns that the teachings of her people, the Seminoles, have a a lot of truth to them.	Aaron (me!) meets Billie as she's hiding from the huge fire. Aaron goes along on the rest of the trip and helps Billie survive the other dangers she encounters.
Cinderella	Poor and mistreated, she still manages to attend the royal party, win the Prince's love, and eventually marry him.	Lisa (me!) is a guest at the King's Ball. Lisa advises Cinderella to leave a little token — like a glass shoe— through which the Prince can find her.

Ask students to use the class chart to rewrite a section of one of the stories to include themselves as part of the action. Students can work independently on this assignment or enlist a partner to help them carry it off.

I watched the Prince dance with a beautiful stranger who was wearing glass shoes! I wondered who she was and why she kept glancing at the clock.

➤ *Writing Prompt!*

Some students may need a "TV-Jog" warm-up. Think of a TV show you like a lot. What episode was particularly interesting? Now imagine that you are an additional character in that episode. Write a narrative paragraph in which *you* take part in the action.

NARRATING PERSONAL CONNECTIONS

Students connect with stories that reflect problems or concerns in their own immediate lives and that at the same time expand their awareness of the universality of those problems or concerns. By narrating these personal connections to literature, students get practice in identifying *theme* in what they read and in thinking about theme as they write their own stories.

LETTERS BETWEEN BOOK CHARACTERS

Purpose: Helps students understand the motives and thoughts of book characters

Have the class brainstorm for a chalkboard list of interesting characters in fiction. The characters may appear in fantasy, sci-fi, historical fiction, fiction set in modern times, or even in narrative poetry. Keep the activity moving fast, offering a suggestion or two of your own if there's a lull in student response.

Robin Hood	Pippi Longstocking	Gulliver
Charlotte	Mafatu	Snow White
Peter Rabbit	Ulysses	Pandora
Amber Brown	Horton (of the egg)	Sherlock Holmes

Discuss the assignment: Imagine that two of the characters on our list can write letters to one another. In the letters, they might tell how their adventures are alike, share feelings, or offer advice. You may wish to present the following example.

Dear Ulysses,

   I admire the way you sail all around for thousands of miles, have scary adventures in strange places, and escape from monsters.

   My adventures all happen in the same place: in Mr. McGregor's garden. I get very scared when he chases me and traps me under watering cans. Can you give me some escape tips?
   Sincerely,
   Peter Rabbit

Dear Peter,

   Thank you for your letter, which was delivered to me at the Cyclops's mailbox. The main thing about escaping from a villain is to have friends who will help you. In my case, I have my faithful crew. In your case, you have your family. I suggest you ask your Mom and Flopsy, Mopsy, and Cotton-Tail to get you out of scrapes.
   Sincerely,
   Ulysses

Ask students to work with a partner. Partners choose two character from different stories, briefly discuss how they're alike and how they're different, and then decide which character each partner will represent. Partner 1 writes the initial letter. Partner 2 reads the letter and writes a response.

WRITING PROCESS IDEA: READ YOUR LETTERS ALOUD

Through a Readers Theater approach, partners can share their letters with classmates. Since partners will read aloud to a large audience, they may wish to briefly rehearse reading slowly, clearly, and with expression. Partners can tell the audience ahead of time what kind of feedback they want. They can reuse previous sharing-and-responding strategies such as say-backs, mental movies, or pointing; or partners may ask the audience to respond by Summarizing: "Listen to hear the main ideas or feelings that our book characters share in their letters. After we read, summarize aloud in your own words what you hear these characters saying in the letters."

> *An audience summary is useful to writers when they want to see if their main ideas are getting through.*

LIFE-EXPERIENCE CONNECTIONS

Purpose: Helps students make connections between their own lives and the experiences of book characters

To the whole class or to a smaller group, present a theme in a book students have recently read. (Note: A theme is stated in a sentence and suggests a universal truth and/or has application to many real-life situations. A book may have more than one theme but choose just one for this activity.) Examples:

BOOK TITLE	A THEME IN THE BOOK
The Moorchild (Eloise McGraw. McElderry 1996)	Sometimes a person feels rejected by everyone around, or so different that she or he doesn't fit in anywhere!
My Brother Sam Is Dead (Collier & Collier. Scholastic 1974)	Family members may strongly disagree with one another about political and social issues.

Ask students to quickly write about a personal experience that is related to the theme. You may wish to call to students' attention that this activity is a form of Quickwrite, in that writers just jot down everything that comes to mind, and will only share their writing if they wish to do so. In this case, however, allow students as much time as they need to complete the activity.

➤ *Writing Prompt!*

If you want to, you can briefly tell a partner about your personal experience before you write about it.

WRITING PROCESS IDEA:
WHISPER-READ, THEN WRITE A SECOND DRAFT

Suggest to students that they quietly read aloud their Personal Experience drafts, making marginal notes about what they'd like to change in a second draft. This is an apt place to review the Composition Skill of Combining Sentences (page 57).

ACTIVITIES

SILENT DIALOGUES

Partners choose a book or story and two characters in it to represent. The students/characters then write notes to one another about big issues or events in the story. Partners may wish to use play-script form.

USING ILLUSTRATIONS

Students choose an illustration in a book they've finished reading, then write freely about all that the illustration shows or predicts about the story.

LITERARY RECIPES

Students choose a book they like, then—using an index card—list the "ingredients" and "directions" the writer has used to "cook" a good story.

CHARACTER ADVERTISEMENTS

Ask students to choose a favorite character from a story, then write and illustrate an advertisement that aims to convince other readers why they'll enjoy reading about the character. Students may want to post their ads on a class bulletin board.

CULMINATING ACTIVITY: WRITING ABOUT LITERATURE

As a class warm-up, review via a chalkboard list the various ways students have explored and written about literature. Examples:

story summaries	Quickwrite impressions	events in order
conversations	new voices	adding events
being in the story	character letters	life experiences

Call on volunteers to tell which activities were the most fun for them or taught them skills they can use as writers.

Ask each student to choose from the Writing Folders two pieces he or she wishes to complete via the writing process. Provide a class period for start-up explorations with these two pieces; that is, the student experiments with the two, then settles on the piece to develop and attaches a tag: "I'm choosing this piece to develop because..." (for example, ...it's almost finished"; ...it's more interesting"; ...it states my ideas very clearly.").

Have pupils polish their drafts, choose writing partners, and use the following rubrics as guidelines in their conferences:

Your Draft Helps Me Really Understand...

	YES	NO	EXAMPLES
1. The story characters			
2. The story plot			
3. How the story is related to real life			

As partners help one another edit, suggest that they pay particular attention to the Composition Skills you've introduced in this section.

Publishing Suggestions:

Read-alouds and Readers Theater may be presented to other classrooms, to families, or in the school or local library. Have the class work on an introduction for the MC to deliver for example: "Our class has been looking at stories as if we were actually in them, or actually taking part in the authors' work. We hope the selections you'll hear will help you understand some of the qualities that make a story appealing to readers."

The presentation might conclude with audience feedback: What have you learned about creating stories?

A Class Anthology titled *Getting Into a Story.* Anthology contents are finished copies of students' work. A small group of students can organize classmates' work, make a Table of Contents, design a cover, and write a brief preface about *Writing Narratives About Literature*. Suggest that all students refer to the anthology for ideas for stories of their own or for new ways to tackle book reports.

PART FOUR

WRITING STORIES

GETTING STARTED

To write original narratives that satisfy them and their readers, students must integrate the elements of characters, plot, and setting. If your students have carried out all or some of the major activities in Parts 1, 2, and 3, they are prepared to investigate these elements in more depth as they write their own stories.

TEACH SKILLS

You may want to integrate the following Composition Skills into this section: Ways to Begin Sentences (page 60); Proofreading Practice (page 61).

START-UP QUICKWRITE

Purpose: Provides a warm-up for planning a story

Fast and furiously, write on this topic: The Most Exciting Thing That Could Ever Happen to a Person. You have five minutes.

INVESTIGATING PLOT: TRADITIONAL STORIES

Purpose: Provides a review of plot-steps

A fairy tale, folktale, myth, or legend with which most of your students are familiar makes a good vehicle for quickly reviewing the components of a plot.

On a chalkboard story-step graphic, stress incidents: (1) the introduction (conflict) incident that tells who the main character is and what she or he wants; (2) the complication incident or incidents that tell how the main character tries to get what she or he wants; (3) the climax incident, or exciting high-point of the story, in which the character either fails or succeeds at solving the problem; (4) the resolution incident, in which the character must face the outcome—satisfactory or unsatisfactory—of the adventure. Example:

Plot Outline for
The Fox and the Grapes

3. Climax: The fox sees that he can never get the grapes.

2. Complication: The fox jumps and jumps again in an attempt to get the grapes.

4. Resolution: The fox decides that the grapes are probably sour anyway, and thus not worth eating.

1. Conflict: A hungry fox spies some grapes, but they're high above him on a vine.

Work with the class, or have partners or small groups work together, to make story steps for other familiar tales. You needn't do a fine-line critique of the story steps. For example, many kids have a hard time initially discerning between complication and climax, or between climax and resolution. The main thing to look for in the story steps is motion: Does the action move along? Are the big events recorded? Does the last step show how the tale ends? Present these broad criteria as you invite students to show their story steps to a larger group, and suggest that they adapt the Free-Read or Mental Movies and strategies (pages 12, 22) to get the kind of feedback they want.

WRITING PROCESS IDEA: CHANGE THE OLD STORY!

Suggest to students that they adapt their story steps to present the fable, fairy tale, or myth to modern times. Start-up examples:

- The fox wants a sandwich at a fast-food store, but he doesn't have any money.
- Rapunzel would like the Prince to rescue her, but she's just cut off most of her hair to achieve a more mod look.
- Icarus has signed up to be the first astronaut to land on Mars, but his Dad (Daedalus) says he's foolish to undertake this dangerous voyage.

➤ *Writing Prompt!*
You've thought of an interesting "modern" plot but don't know where to go from there? Discuss the plot with a classmate to get some ideas about how to proceed.

INVESTIGATE STORY CHARACTERS

Purpose: Helps students focus on characters in a narrative

Many young writers become very adept at settling on the bare-bones of a story plot: this happened, then that happened, and then this is how it ended. The next thing these plot-savvy students want to learn is how to flesh-out these skeleton narratives to make them compelling to readers, just as the authors do in the books these students love. The fleshing-out starts by picturing characters before one begins to write.

Present a Venn diagram that shows the likenesses and differences between key characters in a book students have recently read. Then have students work in groups of five or six to discuss how the plot of the story (the conflict, complications, climax, resolution) grows out of these likenesses and differences. Example:

Main Characters in *My Brother Sam Is Dead*

SAM
- quickly joins the American Revolution defies his father
- will steal to achieve his aims
- quickly takes risks
- never doubts the cause he's fighting for
- is executed by his own army

BOTH
- love their parents
- make hard decisions
- love one another
- suffer in the war

TIM
- follows his parents' loyalty to England
- supports his father
- disapproves of theft
- slowly learns to take risks
- often wonders whose side he's on
- lives to wonder and grieve

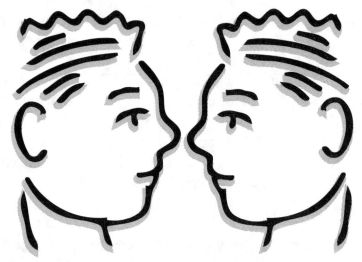

Bring the class together to share the insights of the discussion groups. In general: the exciting incidents in the story grow out of the differences between the main characters and what they want. As a discussion prompt: Imagine that the main characters (Sam and Tim in the example) feel exactly the same way and do exactly the same things. Would the plot be the same? Why not? What are some ways it would change?

WRITING PROCESS IDEA: DESCRIBE TWO CHARACTERS

Ask students to look through their Writing Folders for Parts 1, 2, and 3 of this book to find two characters to describe in a Venn diagram. Emphasize that this is not a final idea for a story, that this is just a fun activity to practice finding likenesses and differences between characters, that choices should be made quickly. (Though don't be surprised if these characters eventually turn up together in students' original stories!) Examples:

The *pigeon* from my Observation Diary (Part 1) and the hawk from my story summary of *My Side of the Mountain*) (Part 3) From Part 2, my grandmother, from my First-Person Biography, and Sojourner Truth, from First-Person Narratives Based on History

Me from my Autobiographical Incident (Part 1) and my dog from If Only They Could Speak (Part 2)

➤ *Writing Prompt!*
Stuck for more ideas about how to fill in your Venn diagram? Ask a partner to look over the Writing Folder notes you're using. Maybe your partner can help you find additional likenesses and differences.

PICTURE THE SETTING

Purpose: Helps students visualize the place where a story happens

The setting of a story has a great deal to do with how characters behave and how they resolve their problems. By guiding students to plan the settings of their own realistic stories, you help them avoid incongruous time-events (such as a futuristic UFO rescuing a right-now cat from a tree) and place-events that jar the reader (such as a farm-child leaving her rural home and immediately boarding a city subway). And even in fantasy stories, the narrative is more convincing if the student has given some prewriting time to thinking about time and place.

As a warm-up, have students work in groups of four or five. Give each group a reproduction of a landscape painting or photograph. (Strive for visual drama: canyons; rugged, snowy mountains; forests; seascapes; aerial views of cities at night, etc.). Ask groups to brainstorm for five minutes or so about events that might happen in that setting. A group scribe can record ideas, then read them to the class as she or he shows the painting or photo. The audience may wish to suggest additional events.

Next, ask each student to draw or paint a picture of the setting of a story he or she is planning to write. Urge kids to include details—for example, not just "a city," but a particular part of a city (tenements? a park? a shopping area?); not just "the country," but a particular part of the countryside (a woodsy picnic ground? a lakeside? a mountain hiking trail?).

WRITING PROCESS IDEA: MAKE A STORY-EVENT MAP

On the setting pictures they've made, students can pencil-in numerals to show in sequence the events that might happen in the setting and provide (again, in pencil) a picture-legend to briefly note these events. (Explain to students that in the process of doing this activity, they may also wish to add details to their pictures! A setting may inspire new story incidents as well as show when and where the original story happens.)

Example: If the picture shows a hiking trail through a woods, the legend might refer in this way to numerals on the picture.

1. Ralph and his dog Louve start here on the trail.
2. This is where Louve spots a deer and runs after it.
3. Ralph gets lost by this stream as he searches for Louve.
4. Ralph huddles under this huge tree as snow starts to fall.
5. This path is where Louve picks up Ralph's scent and follows it.
6. This is the big tree again, where Louve finally finds Ralph.
7. These dotted lines show the route Louve takes to guide Ralph back to the main trail that leads home.

➤ *Writing Prompt!*
You might want to conference with a partner to check whether your picture, numerals, and legend give all the main events in the story you want to write.

GROUP WRITING: STORY PERKS AND STARTERS

Purpose: Provides group input to get stories going

As you know, some students will always drag their heels when it comes to the task of actually writing an original story on their own. The snail's-pace may arise from an honest lack of ideas but just as likely may come from an initial self-judgmental position: *My story has to be perfect from the get-go.* In either case, most hesitant students will find the independent impetus they need from first participating in group writing activities. The Keys: Keep the activities fun and fast. After each activity, offer this Writing Prompt: "If you wish, take some time now to make some notes about how you might "grow" your story."

OBJECT PROMPTS

Ahead of time, prepare a large Grab Bag of 15–20 small items. (Don't give heaps of thought to this, because the activity works best with random items.) Without looking, the student draws 2–4 items from the Grab Bag and then quickly improvises aloud for classmates a brief narrative (three or four good sentences will do) in which the items figure. As follow-up, the audience simply tells what it likes best about the mini-narrative.

Examples of Grab-Bag Items

chalkboard eraser	lunch bag	pencil	flower	textbook
world map	comb	shoe	ruler	mitten
photo of cat	key	mirror	apple	paper clip
movie ticket-stub	compass	clock	twig	postcard

Example of Narrative (You may wish to provide it.)

A hungry cat found a student's old lunch bag. There was just a mitten inside. The cat wrote a postcard to the student. The card said, "If I return your mitten, will you give me something to eat?"

Examples of Positive Audience Comments (You may wish to provide some as models.)

- I like the idea of a cat that can write!
- I like the mystery! Why is a mitten in a lunch bag? How does the cat know who owns the lunch bag?
- I like cats, so I want to know what will happen to a hungry one.

FAMILIAR SAYINGS

On the chalkboard, list some familiar sayings and ask students to briefly explore their meanings by rewording them. Then ask the group to talk about situations in which a character discovers the truth of the saying.

Examples of Sayings and Rewordings

Saying	Rewording
Look before you leap.	Size up what you may be getting into before you do something.
Haste makes waste.	If you do something too fast, you may make mistakes and have to do it all over again.
Many hands make light work.	A big task goes better if lots of people do it together.
A friend in need is a friend indeed.	A true friend is someone who helps you when you're in trouble.

Example of a Situation Based on a Familiar Saying

When I missed a lot of school because I was sick, John, Barbara, and Luis all said, "Don't worry! We'll come by and help you keep up with school assignments." But John was the only one who actually did come by and did help. His actions said a lot more than did Luis's and Barbara's words.

NEW ENDINGS FOR OLD STORIES: GOING ON

Present the traditional endings of stories students are familiar with. Then present "just suppose" alternate endings and encourage students to brainstorm about how to continue the story. Examples:

ENDING	ALTERNATE ENDING	WHAT MIGHT HAPPEN NEXT
The slipper fits, and Cinderella marries the prince.	The slipper fits, but Cinderella declines to marry the prince.	Cinderella decides to open a rental clothing store for party-goers.
The fox can't reach the grapes	The fox finally jumps and gets the grapes	The fox teaches baby foxes how to excel at jumping.
When the queen guesses his name, Rumplestilts-kin disappears.	The queen can't guess his name. Rumplestilts-kin takes the baby.	Rumplestiltskin adopts the baby and teaches him all kinds of great magic tricks.

GREAT BEGINNINGS: GOING ON

Present exciting story-openers and invite students to brainstorm a variety of things that might happen next. Examples:

YOUR OPENER	SAMPLE BRAINSTORM FOLLOW-UPS
As wind howled through the forest, Matt groped his way toward the flickering light in the distance, then stumbled and fell over a weird object.	The object was a skull! Was it human? Maybe this was a warning to stay away.
	The object was a sign that said, "Help!" Maybe someone in the distant cottage needed him.
Laura watched the new girl stumbling through the noisy hallway. The girl was clutching at the wall and muttering angrily to herself.	Laura went up to the girl and said, "What can I do to help you?"
	The angry girl flung open the classroom door of Laura's favorite teacher.
Warmth and peace! These are what the Earth Commanders felt, until they saw the tragic expressions of the beings who came to greet them on this planet of a distant galaxy.	The beings said, "We're glad you have come to rescue us."
	The beings said, "Too bad you've landed here! Now you're in for a dreadful fate.

WRITING PROCESS IDEA: LIST STORY IDEAS IN SEQUENCE

Ask each Group-Writing participant to choose a story the group has discussed—via Object Prompts, Familar Sayings, New Endings, or Great Beginnings—and list in sequence (1,2, 3, etc.) how the narrative might move along from start to finish. Then have students discuss their lists with a partner to determine if the sequence makes sense. Are the steps in order? Are important steps left out?

START YOUR STORY WITH A BANG!

Purpose: Provides a strategy for grabbing the audience's attention and for helping the writer get right into the story

There are all sorts of exceptions of course, but in a model story, the main character, the setting, and an interesting event are presented in the first sentence or paragraph. In writing narratives, as in writing plays, this is called setting the stage. When the stage is set compellingly, the audience wants to read on.

As a warm-up, show the chart that follows, then discuss with the class how the example story-opener combines character, setting, and event.

MAIN CHARACTER	SETTING	FIRST MAIN EVENT
Megan: She is a foster child who feels unloved and unwanted.	An old house in the country, where Megan is living temporarily	Megan sees a ghostly figure in the garden. The figure waves to her.

Lonely and depressed, Megan Stuart kicked her way through the fields around the old house. She knew nobody wanted her. So who was that misty, cloudy person waving to her from the garden in such a friendly way?

Next, present the concept through contrast. Read the following story-openers aloud, then ask students which one best grabs their attention, and why it does so. (Most students will choose the first, because it focuses on the big event, presents the main character in action, leaves out minor details, and is exciting.)

1. A picnic was never supposed to be like this! Running from the horrendous heat of the forest fire, Lucas suddenly remembered that his little sister, Dina, was back there by the picnic ground—all alone! Lucas conquered his fear in a burst of love and doubled-back through the searing heat to rescue Dina.

2. Lucas and his family went out for a picnic in the country. While his family packed up to go home, Lucas went exploring. His little sister, Dina, stayed at the picnic table, playing with her Barbies. Meanwhile, Lucas ran into a forest fire started by some careless camper. He was very fearful. Then he remembered that Dina was in danger. So he went back to the picnic ground and rescued her.

On a chart, present characters, settings, and initial events. Students can work independently or with a partner to draft exciting story-openers that combine these elements.

Examples:

MAIN CHARACTER	SETTING	FIRST MAIN EVENT
A Bear: He was born in the woods, but has lost his way.	a shopping mall parking lot at night	A shopper returns to her car and finds the bear sitting on it.
A Railroad Engineer: He's an old-timer who thinks he's seen everything.	a lonely stretch of track in the middle of nowhere	A woman bursts into the engineer's cab and insists that he stop the train immediately.
A Clown: She is on her way to a circus in a distant city.	A plane is having trouble in a thunderstorm.	Some passengers begin to freak out with fear.

WRITING PROCESS IDEA: DRAFT YOUR STORY'S OPENER

Ask students to use what they've learned to write an opening paragraph for their original stories. To self-critique their drafts, students might ask an audience to respond through Mental Movies (p. 22) or Pointing (p. 34). Another strategy writers and audience might use is Almost-Said. The writer asks the audience: "What did you hear sort of hinted-at in my story opener? What would you like to know more about?"

Almost-Said provides writers with new ideas, and also serves as a check-point to inform writers whether or not their story-beginnings are engaging audience interest.

ACTIVITIES

PARALLEL SENTENCES

Present story-openers, underlining key words and phrases. Students copy the openers, substituting their own ideas for the ones you've underlined. Example:

- In the dark and gloomy forest, Drusilla looked for something to eat.
- In the noisy and crowded school, Drusilla looked for someone to be her friend.

POETRY

Encourage students to browse through poetry anthologies to find story ideas. Narrative poems, like "The Highway Man" or "Mending Walls," are an immediate source, but writers can also find story inspirations in lyric poems like "The Moon's the North Wind's Cookie" and "Fog."

MUSIC

You can preface, then play, compositions that are frankly narrative, such as "Til Eulenspighel" or "Pictures at an Exhibition," then ask students to trans-

late the musical narrative into written narrative. You can also play "mood" pieces, such as "La Mer" and "Moonlight Sonata," and ask kids to note story ideas that come to them as they listen.

ART
Ask students to draw a picture of an event from their own lives. Students exchange pictures with a partner, and the partner writes a story based on what he or she sees in the picture.

CULMINATING ACTIVITY: WRITING A STORY
Review with the class the components, or criteria, of a good story. Summarize the ideas and post them so that students can refer to them as they draft, conference, and revise. Example:

COMPONENTS OF A GOOD STORY
1. Characters:
The main character has a problem to solve.
The characters are believable and interesting.

2. Plot:
The events are told in the order they happen.
All the important steps are included.
The plot makes sense.

3. Setting:
It's clear to the reader where and when the story takes place.

4. Language:
The writer uses vivid, exact words.

Suggest that as a prewriting strategy, the student briefly discuss story plans with a partner. Partners might share the Writing Folder notes they will use to build their stories.

After partners conference to determine if the general criteria (above) have been met in their drafts, the writer may want to ask for more specific feedback. Examples:
- "I want to make (character's name) really funny and likeable. Does this come across? Do you have any suggestions?"
- "Close your eyes as I read this section. Tell me what you see in your mind's eye."
- "Tell me what the strongest parts of my story are. What do you think makes them strong."

Before students revise, remind them that a great many professional writers make several drafts of a story before they hammer out the final copy. While your students need not write a series of drafts, they should be allowed a couple of class periods to refine parts of their stories, perhaps testing out the refinements with their writing partners.

The class can brainstorm for publishing ideas. Examples:
- A class *Short Story Anthology*
- Individual books, with covers and illustrations
- Dramatizations of stories:
    Readers Theater
    Scripting and acting a play based on a story
- A *Writers' Best* newsletter for families and other classrooms in which each student selects for publication a story passage that he or she is particularly proud of
- Read-alouds to present in classrooms or in the library
- Authors' Lunch: Your writers take turns as speakers at a class lunch time conference.
    Each speaker tells briefly:
        - the problems encountered in writing a story;
        - the fun of story-writing;
        - about the next stories he or she would like to write.

PART FIVE

COMPOSITION SKILLS

REPRODUCIBLES

Suggestions about when to use each of the reproducibles in Part 5 are given in *Getting Started*. Have students follow up the review by using the Composition Skill to revise or edit pieces from their Writing Folders

Suggest that students keep completed Composition Skills pages in a reference section of their Writing Folders.

Name _____

STRONG VERBS

A strong verb is a verb with muscles. All alone, it can carry just as much, or even more meaning than a string of weaker words. Examples:

(Pretty weak!): The lights <u>shine off and on</u> in the distance as the little boat <u>moves from side to side</u> in the water.

(Strong!): The lights <u>glimmer</u> in the distance as the little boat <u>drifts</u> in the water.

A. Find a strong verb in the box to use in place of the underlined words in the sentence. Write the new sentence.

1. She <u>looked angrily</u> at me.
2. The fire <u>made little noises</u>.
3. We <u>looked very closely at</u> the moth.
4. He <u>held</u> the bat <u>tightly</u>.
5. They <u>called very loudly</u>.
6. She <u>walked slowly</u> in the garden.

crackled	glared	gripped	strolled	hollered	studied

B. Use a dictionary or thesaurus to find the meanings of the strong verbs below. Then write a sentence using each verb.

1. bother, fluster
2. swagger, prance
3. coax, plead
4. admire, appreciate

C. Choose at least five strong verbs from activities **A** and **B** above. Write a brief narrative paragraph in which you use the five verbs.

_____
_____
_____
_____
_____
_____

PRECISE NOUNS

Precise means accurate, exact. Think of a precise noun as a camera with an accurate, exact focus. The precise noun delivers a word-picture that shows the reader exactly what you mean. Examples:

There was a lot of stuff on the shelves.

There was a variety of toys on the shelves.

Find a precise noun in the box to use in place of the underlined words.

1. He faced <u>a lot of hard things</u> bravely.
2. We had an interesting <u>fight</u> about politics.
3. She stared in <u>surprise</u> at the Grand Canyon.
4. They found <u>little pieces of things</u> from the meteorite.
5. I've reached the <u>general idea</u> that writing can be fun.

awe	hardships	fragments	conclusion	argument

Use a dictionary or thesaurus to find the important differences in meaning in each pair of nouns below. Then write sentences that show the different meanings precisely.

1. terror, panic   3. secret, mystery   5. promise, agreement

2. mixture, blend   4. form, outline   6. shock, amazement

Search through your Writing Folder to find a piece of writing that you could improve by making some of the nouns precise. Rewrite the piece. Share the original and your rewrite with a partner.

TRANSITIONAL WORDS

Transitional words link related ideas and hold them together. Think of a train and the links that hold the cars together. Some transitions, or links, connect events to show when they happen.

| Marty recognized the puppy | as soon as | he saw it | and immediately | picked it up. |

Some transitions link related thoughts on a subject.

| The puppy shivered | because | it was afraid | even though | Marty spoke in a gentle voice. |

CONTINUE THE STORY IN YOUR OWN WAY

Go on with the story of Marty and the puppy. Write one or more paragraphs in which you use at least six transitional words and phrases. You may use the ones above, as well as the following:

Time Transitions			Thought Transitions		
after	earlier	meanwhile	also	mainly	therefore
before	eventually	next	if	otherwise	unless
during	finally	then	like	since	furthermore
while	when	now	which	also	even though

_____

_____

_____

_____

_____

COMBINING SENTENCES

You can state a Big Idea in one sentence, for example:

I admire my grandfather.

You can go on to support this main idea with more sentences:

I admire him because he is always helping people.

The people need jobs, homes, or food.

There's a more effective way to build the Big Idea: combine it with the supporting ideas to make one sentence:

I admire my grandfather because he is always helping people who need jobs, homes, or food.

Combine each sentence group below to make one sentence. Example:

I'll never forget that sunny day. We went to the park.

I'll never forget that sunny day when we went to the park.

(**Hint:** Use transitional words, like those listed on page 56.)

1. Clouds began to move in. The day suddenly turned cool.

_____

2. The rain began. We had to dash for shelter.

_____

3. We went into the bandstand. It was empty. It had a big roof.

_____

4. We ate our lunches there. The rain pattered down. Thunder boomed.

_____

5. We enjoyed our picnic. The rain was quite a surprise!

_____

Search through your Writing Folder to find a narrative that you could improve by combining some of the sentences. Rewrite the piece and share it with a group of classmates.

COMPARISONS

A *comparison* tells your readers how one thing is like another.
To keep your readers interested, avoid ho-hum, tired comparisons such as:

quiet as a mouse   **white as snow**   **silly as a clown**

Strive for original comparisons of your very own. Examples:

quiet as a spider on silk   **white as a ghost in a snowstorm**

silly as a guppy's giggle

Complete each comparison below in your own way. Then share your comparisons with your classmates.

1. loud as a _____   **4.** soft as a _____

2. sad as a _____   **5.** happy as a _____

3. fast as _____   **6.** slow as _____

The word like is often used in comparisons. In many cases, though, you may want to leave out like to make a more powerful comparison. Examples:

The ancient tree was ~~like~~ the wise old man of the forest.

The hailstones were ~~like~~ frozen bullets.

Write a sentence that compares each thing below to something else.
Don't use the word like.

1. a wrecked, deserted house

_____

2. a wild and stormy sea

_____

3. a leaf in the wind

_____

4. new flowers in springtime

_____

Look through your Writing Folder to find a narrative that you could improve by using comparisons. Rewrite the narrative. Read it aloud to a classmate.

PUNCTUATING CONVERSATION

In your narratives, you may often want to tell, or quote, the exact words, or direct quotations, of a character. The chart below shows six punctuation rules to follow.

DON'T-WORRY NOTE: Don't worry about these rules too much as you draft your narratives. Do use the rules as you edit and proofread with a writing partner.

	RULE	EXAMPLE
1.	Put quotation marks around the exact words of the person. Capitalize the first word.	Aunt Em said, "Here's my photo album."
2.	Use a comma to set off the quotation from the rest of the sentence.	I said, "I'd like to look at it."
3.	Put a period, question mark, or exclamation mark inside the quotation mark.	She said, "Do you recognize any of these people?" "No!" I said.
4.	Sometimes a quotation is divided. *If the quote makes one sentence, put the first comma inside the first part, and the second comma outside the second part. *If the divided quote makes two sentences, begin the second sentence with a capital letter.	"This is your grandpa," said Aunt Em, "and this is me!" "Well," I said, "you look like me!" "Photo albums are fun," I said. "These pictures tell me about my family."
5.	If you're quoting more than one speaker, begin each speaker's words with a new paragraph.	—-"Aren't you studying family histories in school?" —-"We sure are!" I said.
6.	Don't confuse direct quotations with indirect quotations. In a direct quotation, the writer expresses the speaker's exact words. Don't use quotation marks in indirect quotations.	"I'll let you take this album to school," said Aunt Em. "First promise me you'll keep it safe!" May aunt said I could take the album to school if I promised to keep it safe.

WAYS TO BEGIN SENTENCES

To get your readers interested in your narrative, begin your sentences with words and phrases that capture attention!

Sometimes the subject is the attention-getter and should come first. Example:
The three abandoned kittens looked for food.

Sometimes description is the attention-getter. Put the description first. Example:
In the howling wind and cold rain, the kittens sought shelter.

Sometimes actions are the attention-getters and should come first. Example:
Mewing and crying, the kittens longed for their mother.

A. The attention-grabber is underlined in each sentence.
Rewrite the sentence to put the attention-grabber first. Example:

I see a lot of <u>lost pets</u> roaming around in our city.

Rewrite: <u>Lost pets</u> roam around in our city.

1. There was an empty lot, and <u>a skinny dog</u> scrounged around in it.

_____

2. The hungry dog was <u>sniffing at cans and papers</u> trying to find something to eat.

_____

3. The dog yelped and ran away <u>when some mean kids threw rocks at it</u>.

_____

B. On a separate sheet of paper, rewrite the following paragraph to make the sentences open in ways that are more likely to grab the readers' attention.

I've always wanted a dog, so I called the dog to me. I saw that the dog was scared and cautious because it crept toward me slowly. I held out my hand and as I did that, the dog came closer. I spoke softly to it, and then the dog wagged its tail. I took the dog home, and now we are getting used to each other.

C. Find a narrative in your Writing Folder that you can improve by beginning sentences in audience-grabbing ways. Rewrite the narrative.
Read it aloud to classmate.

Name _____

PROOFREADING PRACTICE

1. Use the proofreader's marks below.
2. Note the correction in the line *and* in the right-hand margin.
3. If possible, use a colored pencil.

≡ **Capitalize**

∧ **Add a word or words**

(Sp) **Correct the spelling**

⊙ **Add a period**

? **Add a question mark**

! **Add an exclamation mark**

∧ **Add a comma**

ℓ **Take out a word**

Example

(SP) I imagined myself as a (charater) in My Side of the mountain. What if I met Sam as I was hiking in the forest? Would

(?) we become friends. That would depend on I had as much **whether** courage common sense, and curiosity as as Sam does.

Practice: Proofread each of the following sentences.

1. I don't have a lot of wilderness eperience, but I'm willing learn.

2. As for curioisty I believe I've got plenty. I'd be interested in everything sam had had to teach me.

3. What about courage. I'm not sure, but I think we only find out how couragos we are when we're a tough situation.

Apply what you know: Work with a partner. Proofread some samples from your Writing Folders.

NOTES

NOTES